Jamila Finds a Friend

by Alison Hawes

illustrated by
Marcin Piwowarski

CAMBRIDGE
UNIVERSITY PRESS

UCL
Institute of Education

T0373852

Jamila finds a book.

Jamila finds a pencil.

Jamila finds a ruler.

Jamila finds a ball.

Jamila finds a doll.

Jamila finds a banana.

Jamila finds a friend!

14

Jamila Finds a Friend Alison Hawes

Teaching notes written by Sue Bodman and Glen Franklin

Using this book

Developing reading comprehension

This simple cumulative story supports development of early print concepts: that print carries meaning and is read from left to right.

Grammar and sentence structure

- A simple one line repetitive sentence structure that includes the high-frequency word 'a' and introduces a new familiar, highly-redundant new word on each page.
- Some early opportunity to explore how punctuation aids expression when reading.

Word meaning and spelling

- Simple one-line text to attempt and practise one-to-one correspondence.
- Matching across a line of print, locating known words.
- Use of initial letter cues to cross-check with other information in print to problem-solve new words.

Curriculum links

Geography – Simple mapping of routes around the school or in the playground and what children find there.

Maths – Cumulative story. How many objects did Jamila find? What if she found two rulers? Three books?

Citizenship – Explore nature of friendship. Who is your friend?

Learning outcomes

Children can:

- understand that print carries meaning and is read from left to right
- attempt and practise one-to-one correspondence
- read a range of familiar and common sentences independently
- read and write a high-frequency word.

A guided reading lesson

Book Introduction

Give a book to each child and read the title.

Orientation

Give a brief overview of the book, using the verb in the same form as it is in the text:

In this book, a little girl is walking to school with her mum. She finds lots of things on the way. Let's look at what she finds.

Preparation

Draw attention to the repetitive sentence structure:

Page 2: *Look here* (point to the picture). *What does Jamila find? Yes, Jamila finds a book. Let's read together* (encourage children to point and read sentence on page 2).

Page 4: *Now what does she find?*

Carry on through the book with the children looking at pictures and discussing the items Jamila finds. Establish that children have noticed the items falling from the rucksack.